Heavenly Realm Publishing

Houston, Texas

Published By: Heavenly Realm Publishing
P. O. Box 682532, Houston, TX 77268
www.heavenlyrealmpublishing.com
Toll Free 1-866-216-0696

Printed in the United States of America

ISBN—13: 9781937911-73-7 (paperback)
ISBN—13: 9781937911-74-4 (ebook)

Library of Congress Cataloging-in-Publication Data: 2016905616
Stephanie Franklin
The Peacemaker: *Avoiding & Resolving Conflicts Within Relationships & the Church*/ Stephanie Franklin

Religion—Christian Life—General. United States. **2.** Religion—Christian Life—Relationships—United States. **3.** Religion—Christian Church—General —United States.

This book is printed on acid free paper.

Scripture quotations are from the Holy Bible King James version. All rights reserved.

Stephanie Franklin
Stephanie Franklin Ministries
info@stephaniefranklinministries.org
www.stephaniefranklin.org

THE

PEACE MAKER

*Avoiding & Resolving
Conflicts Within Relationships,
the Church & in the Work Place*

Stephanie Franklin

Books by Stephanie

Novels
1. When Ramona Got Her Groove Back from God
2. My Song of Solomon
3. My Song of Solomon *Prayer Journal*
4. God Loves *Thugs* Too!

Marriage & Relationships
1. *Winning Together: His Needs Matter, Her Needs Are Important*

Family & Relationships, Youth
1. *Winning Together As a Parent: Loving Each Other While Knowing Your Children and Teen Is Included and Not Separate.*

Children
1. *The Purpose Chaser: For Children Ages 5 to 12*

Ministry & Faith Inspirational
1. Position Your Faith for Great Success
2. Position Your Faith for Great Success Workbook
3. *The Peacemaker: Avoiding & Resolving Conflicts Within Relationships & the Church*
4. Church Hurt: *How to Heal & Overcome It*
5. *The Power of the Healing*
6. *The Power of the Holy Spirit*
7. DO it ON PURPOSE

Sports & Fitness Motivational
1. The Locker Room Experience: *For the Struggling Athlete & Coach, & Tips on How to Get Recruited in Sports*
2. RE*shape* YOU: *A Fitness Guide to Teach You How to Create the NEW YOU from the Inside Out.*
3. RE*shape*YOU *Elderly Fitness Exercises & Eating Plan Book*

THE PEACEMAKER

Avoiding & Resolving Conflicts Within Relationships, the Church & in the Work Place

- ❖ Listen before you speak is where you win
- ❖ 1/4 percent you, 1/3 percent them
- ❖ Seek to understand rather than to agree
- ❖ Seek a plan of action

Preface

Peacemakers are those who have the heart of God. They are the ones who strive to make peace even when it is not before them. They are ready to forgive and to forget. Peacemakers are those who know they are not perfect and have literally found out that they too are not worthy and are not perfect.

The Peacemaker has come to encourage those who may be struggling in this area of peacemaking and failing in the area of conflict with others.

God loves when we as people can take off our masks, be real about our struggles, and expose the truth about our imperfections. Then we can promote love, encouragement, peace, forgiveness, restoration, reconciliation, and fairness toward one another when needed. He can trust us and delight in using us for His glory. Are you apart of the team of peacemakers? Are you making peace whenever and wherever disagreement and conflict should arise? Strive to be a peacemaker as you journey through *The Peacemaker*.

"Blessed are the peacemakers: for they shall be called the children of God."

Matthew 5:9

Introduction

We define the word *conflict* as a serious disagreement or comment. Normally in relationships, church conflicts or work place conflicts, we can say that the word "conflict" and its meaning would best fit as someone's disagreement with another's words, actions, or attitude.

Words are more damaging than someone physically striking someone. A physical punch can heal over time, but a damaging word or a bunch of negative words can damage for a lifetime. No one can bring those words back. The person who said them may apologize, but they still

Words are more damaging than someone physically striking someone.

may never erase them from the wounded person's heart. God has called each of us to forgive a person seven times seventy times per day (Matthew 18:22). This may seem unreal in this day and time, but it is true. It may seem like a hard thing to do when in the line of conflict, but if you were the victim instead of the villain, you would run to forgive. As a result of the conflict, the wounded victim is left damaged. The power of the tongue is a killer. It can take a person out in a matter of minutes. I have seen this happen during my years of serving in ministry in the church. There have been sisters and brothers in the church, who at first seem to be getting along while making Christ-like decisions for the individual ministries they serve in, and next seeing them in the line of conflict for control for position and a heated battle to be right. *The Peacemaker* comes to bring Biblical knowledge of what the Bible says about how to resolve conflict within these types of relationships. It helps the reader to understand that they are not the only ones on this earth, in the church, in the work place and that it is important and vital to work together to fulfill God's Kingdom assignment while here on earth.

Words can be tragic and can lose someone's life. I have witnessed this on the local news where someone heard that the other party said some untrue things and wanted to get back at them, well, their retaliation was not just a punch in the mouth, it turned out deadly as to them murdering the one who spoke the words whether untrue or not. These types of conflicts can be avoided if people would come together and pray for their city, work place, school, neighborhood, state, nation, and world. While none of us can run from conflict, we can all come together, pray and work together in unity. And, if conflict arises, we are equipped and can nip it in the bud by peacefully and respectfully talking about it; and come to a peaceful resolution without fighting, bickering, and without a negative outcome.

The whole idea here is to agree to disagree. You may not agree with what one another say at times, however, you have to respect how they feel. You cannot change a person, only that person can change themselves so you might as well respect them and move on.

Actions speak louder than words. Actions have caused many to leave this earth before it was their time. In Biblical terms, if we look at the Israelites under the leadership of Moses, as Moses led them out of Egypt by way of obedience to God's commands (Exodus 14:10-31), they complained, murmured, and wanted the old life rather than the blessings and the blessed land that God had planned for them. They could not see the promise for looking at their current circumstances. They were very harsh and unbelieving with their words and actions. As a result, many did not see the promise land (land of Canaan). You cannot allow your feelings and emotions to control your words and actions and make you sin. As we look at the church. There are situations where because there were conflict among the members, they have either departed with negative choice words, not choosing to sit next to each other, angrily chose to sit down instead of serving in the place of ministry God called them to, stopped coming to church but kept their name on the church roll, sowed seeds of discord by discouraging other members from serving in the church, left the church completely, or involved others outside of the church that came in the church and made a big commotion. All of this negative commotion is due to wrong decision-making, selfish opinions, and damaging actions that made the outcome very detrimental. Actions must be controlled on a daily basis by disciplining yourself to not sin by lashing out at the person(s) who hurt you or made you mad. It is not easy at times, in fact, it would sometimes seem impossible when in the face of someone who refuses to respect you, act right, and submit to a peacemaking agreement. But, it can be done. It has to be done. If not, the outcome will always be you going home with a big headache, or sitting in jail for something that could have been avoided.

Attitude plays a big part in your relationship(s) whether on a personal level, in your community, or in the church. With the wrong attitude, disagreements can quickly occur. I have never seen a right, positive attitude bring disagreement. Jesus had the right attitude. He was on a mission with a Kingdom assignment. On the other hand, the children of Israel had the wrong attitude when following leadership and the Lord. They did not want to follow authority; all they wanted to do was complain and do things their way. How many of us are like that? Are you like that? Are you hard to please? Do people shun from your presence? Have anybody ever given you a blessing and you received it as if it were a curse? Attitude plays a big part in whether or not you are promoted on your job, or work in a peaceful environment with your co-worker(s). It plays a big part in whether or not you get married or remain married. It plays a big part in whether or not you will be effective and happy in friendships and/or relationships. It plays a big part in whether or not you make a great mother/grandmother or father/grandfather. Attitudes matter in everything you do, everywhere you go, and the people you come in contact with. So make sure you are always on guard, not allowing the enemy to steal and destroy; and make people falsely accuse you when you're really an innocent and a nice person.

The Peacemaker Questions to Ask Yourself

1. When it is appropriate to overlook an offense
2. How to change attitudes and habits that lead to conflict
3. How to confess wrongs honestly and effectively
4. When to assert your rights
5. How to correct others effectively
6. How to forgive others and achieve genuine reconciliation
7. How to negotiate just and reasonable agreements
8. How to deal with people who refuse to be reasonable
9. How to use conflict as an opportunity to demonstrate the love and power of Jesus Christ
10. When to ask the church to intervene in a conflict

THE

PEACE MAKER

Avoiding & Resolving
Conflicts Within Relationships,
the Church & in the Work Place

Compromise can heal all peacemaking situations.

—Stephanie Franklin

1

You Cannot Run from Conflict, It is Everywhere

- Connection plays a huge role at avoiding conflict
- There are different levels in conflicts
- Quietly Listening, Actively Listening, and Critical Listening

Connection Plays a Huge Role at Avoiding Conflict

Connecting with people in a positive way plays a huge role at avoiding conflict. Connecting works best when giving and taking, and taking and giving. You give and they take, they give and you take. One is releasing while the other is receiving and vice-versa. You both are sharing the floor. No one is left out, and no one feels that his or her ideas or opinions are unimportant.

> **You can learn a lot when you quietly listen to the other person.**

You can learn a lot when you quietly listen to the other person. Successful relationships are built on listening, followed by reacting. There are times when reacting is not necessary, listening is more important. Most conflicts derive from lack of listening, controlling the conversation, and refusing to forgive the other person for what they did or said. For example, if a person is angry about something that happened in the past, whether near or far, their attitude and will to listen is contaminated by what they are still angry about and are not admitting. They will control the conversation and the person in order to get their way, and for them to only see their point as if their point is the only thing that matters. This alone will cause the other person to not listen, become angry, take the conversation for granted, and have an unconcern attitude. You can never have a successful relationship with these types of attitudes and actions. The result of these ways are separation, physically fighting, verbally duking it out with their words, divorce, abuse, jail time, and/or even death.

You cannot run from conflict, it is everywhere. However, how you handle it is what's important. Where most fail is they try to handle conflict in a negative way. You can only win in conflict with a winning and positive attitude. Your attitude should be that you are determined to win no matter what, and the outcome is going to be victorious.

Your goal should be to:

1. **Stay calm** no matter what (even if they are yelling, pacing, and even showing some physical action but not hitting).
2. **Stay focus** (keep your thoughts on winning in the conversation, argument, or heated battle).
3. **Listen** as much as you can before making your point. The Bible states something that is so true and so profound if followed. Look in James 1:19, where James states in scripture about being *quick to hear and slow to speak and slow to wrath* (anger). It is important to be a peacemaker as much as you can, while at the same time being realistic and not over doing it; and not with being phony as if it doesn't matter or you're not hurt so you refuse to listen.

Conflict is exposed when the one in the relationship does not quietly listen. Most people who share, want the listening party to actively listen to what they have to say instead of jumping to add their opinion or make a comment. It takes two to argue. A person cannot argue by themselves. However, if the person who you are in conflict with becomes extremely angry and goes off on you, you are not obligated to do the same. I have failed so many times in this area in the past. It is one of the hardest things to do when the heated party is right before you, in your face yelling while egging you on to fight them back. But, if you want to win in every conflict and make the devil out of a liar, you MUST set a goal and learn to do the points I just stated above.

There Are Different Levels of Conflicts.

There are different levels in conflicts.

1. Simple Conflicts
2. Extreme Conflicts
3. Detrimental Conflicts

Simple conflicts happen when there are two or more persons arguing over something very minor. This usually is a case where the conflict should not have happened, or should not be happening in the first place. For example, arguing over who gets the last free give-a-way available at a workshop. Another example is two couples arguing over what to cook at home. And last, two friends ordering ice cream, argue over what kind of ice cream to order. These examples usually turns into heated arguments which are not necessary. I have learned that no one can make no one do what they do not want to do, nor make them say what they do not want to say. If you notice in the first example, there is a glitch and the glitch is selfish control? Yes, selfish control. It does not matter who gets the last free give-a-way pencil to use at a workshop. I'm sure there are many other options, like using a pen you or someone already has that can be used just as effectively as well. Everything should be done in order, in order to keep peace at all times. Before the workshop begins, two or more should decide how the workshop is going to run and what supplies are going to be given-a-way free; and make sure there is more than enough to give-a-way so no one is left out.

Extreme conflicts happen when there is a point where the incident of conflict seems to be resolved, however, one of the parties involved brings it back up or allows it to die down and resurrects it again. Most times this comes from excessive anger or their struggle to forgive with the feeling within of, "I can't believe what you did to me." Or "I can't forgive you for what you did to me or against me." Or even, "I want to make you angry because you hurt me." Or lastly, "I want to hurt you because you hurt me." These are extreme conflicts that can only be resolved when you forgive and allow yourself to take each day at a time to remove the festered hurt of anger and hatred, and unforgiveness within. When you conquer this, you will be able to look at the person you had conflict with and feel no parts of anger, hatred, resentment, or unforgiveness in your heart.

Detrimental conflicts happen when there is an aftermath of cop and ambulance vehicles leaving the scene with someone in it. Conflict and detrimental battles occur to the degree when someone have reached their limit and have lost control in such a way that someone has become an injured victim or an expired victim. This brings me to think of Cain and Abel in Genesis 4:1-16. Cain became very angry and jealous of Abel because the Lord received Abel's offering and not his. As a detrimental result, Cain attacked and killed Abel his brother over something foolish. Cain's conflict did not look at how he could find a way to please the Lord after the Lord made His decision. However, instead, Cain took it upon himself to take vengeance out on his brother and take him out. Have you ever seen this type of detrimental conflict in your life? What about someone else's life? Have you ever been a victim of this type of detrimental conflict yourself? Have you ever seen this type in your workplace? This type of detrimental conflict happens all over the world—in our homes, neighborhoods, communities, schools, on our jobs, and even in the church. There have been many cases where conflict has happened in the church and the person who was picked on or persecuted against, came back and got revenge either on the administration, the pastor, minister, deacon, sister in the church, brother in the church, youth, young adult, or even someone's child. Also, there have been cases where the person who was like Cain in the church, committed worse crimes in the church, school, or even on the job as well. Cain was very jealous of his brother and allowed his rage of jealousy and the fact that he was not favored or respected to control his mind in so that he crossed the boundaries of right, and allowed the devil to make him kill his very own biological brother. In order to break this cycle of conflict, the Christian Believer should stay on his or her knees praying peace always between the people of this world. There has to be a level of prayer going forth, not only within the church of one Believer, but within the entire Body of Christ of many Believers on a constant, daily basis. Who's to say it won't be you next? Who's to say it won't be you involved in a heated battle that turns detrimental? No one wants to ever be put in that position or those positions, but the devil is shrewd and has a way of tempting those who are weak, and turn someone or something good into a whole new detrimental life changing moment. God forbid, but this is the truth and it has happened all over the world.

There was a time, years ago, I was at a friend's gathering and there seemed to be nothing that could make the gathering go wrong—no potential fighting or arguing, no negative cliquish gatherings, and everybody was having a good time and appeared to be happy with one another. It all changed in a quick moment when a familiar person they all knew came with another person, alcohol became the highlight, and arguing turned into physical fighting; and one thing led to another. The final aftermath was someone got shot and badly injured until a point of death. When detrimental conflict is avoided by going your separate way before the argument begins, this area will be no more and peace and harmony can prosper everywhere. Remember, it takes two to argue. No one can argue by him or herself. It would look very funny if tried. So with that in mind, walk away. Do not allow your feelings to get the best of you. Think before you react. If you know you're going to a place where a person who either does not like you, or you do not like them, do not go there. You will open the door to potential conflict that may not have a positive outcome. Seek the advice of someone who is strong in the area of conflict who can help you make the right decisions and keep you calm if in the mist of battle that is not your fault.

I do not believe that I have ever heard of anyone who has never gotten angry, or have never lost control at one point in time in his or her life. I have ministered and prayed with enough families and people to know that there are not very many. In fact, that is the hot topic most times. I myself have gotten angry and have lost control to a point where I regret some of the things I did and said, I'm sure we all have. However, there has to be a point in all of our lives where we have to come together and help one another to resolve these areas that the enemy loves to pick on. He loves heated battles. In fact, he specializes in many rooted, underground areas within this tree. Nevertheless, the Christian Believer can be victorious in these areas of battle, even if you have made mistakes in the past. Make today your day that you are no longer going to be bound and a victim to the devil using you to bring either negative conflicts, or being in position to succumb to negative conflicts.

Do not allow people to control you to make you lose control to a point where you lose who you are, and become somebody else. And, after it is all over, and you've done the damage, you have to ask yourself either, "why did I do that?" or "What was I thinking?"

Quietly Listening, Actively Listening, and Critical Listening

These three topics show action toward listening quietly, actively listening, and critical listening.

Quietly listening is considered as action. You must actively listen as the other person is actively expressing themselves. Two people cannot talk at the same time effectively. One must submit while the other goes forth. If this is abused and lines are crossed, conflict happens. The problem here is that both persons want to talk at the same time. Impossible. This is not a healthy conversation. Someone will always get offended or feel over powered. This is why in the Bible there were never two kings at the same time. There can only be one person to lead and the other must follow until, if ever, it is the other person's time to lead and go forth. It is a together thing. They two are connected together. Disconnection cannot be a part of this impartation.

Actively listening occur when the person who is listening to the other person is writing down or typing what is being said to them. They are actively listening. For example, in a workshop or meeting, there is a mediator, a proctor, or a teacher who is speaking, teaching, and giving instructions. He or she is supplying important information to those who are actively listening by writing notes or typing notes in their tablets, laptops, or on their notepads, etc. In order to effectively receive, you have to effectively listen. You cannot obtain information while talking at the same time, or by cutting off the one who is supplying the information to you. Often time's relationships are torn a part because one of the persons will not listen to what the other person has to say to them. I have been a victim of this and also have been guilty as well either way. It will benefit both parties to be a peacemaker by listening to the fullness before giving your feedback. This is the key to having an understanding, loving, strong prosperous relationship. I share this in my book, *"Winning Together"*. There may be times when you feel as if you just have to say something because the other person either says something you do not agree with, or they talk too much, too long, or will not allow you to get a word in edge wise. You should still listen to them until they have completely finished what they have to say or until they ask you a question. By hearing them out completely and they doing the same to you, allows you to add your part by saying what you have to say in a peaceful manner and not being interrupted. This has to be practiced by both parties in order for it to be effective. As a result, this resolves and keeps conflict(s) away. It should be your goal to keep out conflict and let peace be the center of the conversation, and yours, and their life each day. While none of us are perfect, you and those who you are having a challenge with should strive to perfect this area if you want to see positive change and have a peaceful respectful relationship.

Remember:
1. Actively listen without interrupting them.
2. Write down questions or comments you want to ask or comment on while they are sharing what they have to say.
3. When they have completed what they have to say, ask and make your comments from what you wrote down, as they do not interrupt you.

4. Give them a chance to answer your questions and comments without you interrupting them.

5. You two come to an agreement and respect for how you both feel before departing from each other, or changing the subject and moving on.

Critical Listening comes when it is to death that you listen to a person. What I mean by this is, there have been times when a person have over talked the other person who really needed them to listen. And because they didn't, the person who needed the listening ear, either committed suicide or something very critical happened to them. Also, another example is when a person who needed the other person to listen and they did not, and as a result the other person missed out on a life changing blessing and a supernatural answer to their prayers. There are seasons to everything and you can miss your season by operating in pride, control, over talking them, not listening, and/or allowing others or things to distract you. They can make you have to wait a very long time for the life changing season to come again. While God cannot lie, He has to fulfill His every promise; the enemy can hinder and use this stumbling block to set your time back further. It is critical that you listen. Your important information may not come from those who you are familiar with, or it may not come from the one who always seem to make you smile, or from the one who always talk to you. It just may come from the homeless person on the street panhandling, or the worse person you do not want to see. So, do not take listening to another person for granted, it can also save your life.

2

How to Control Your Anger in the Heat of Conflict

Conflict is everywhere. All over the world, we hear about conflict. If you look at your local news broadcast, you will see conflict. If you look at television, you will see conflict. If you look around you, you will see conflict. You will see it on the streets as a another vehicle cuts you off for no apparent reason, somebody pushing their shopping cart into yours without apologizing, the church judging you,

> *Controlling your anger in the heat of battle is not the easiest thing to do.*

and someone on your job lying on you for no apparent reason. I have learned that the world leans on conflict. If a television show does not have conflict in it, it will be replaced with another that does. If a movie does not have conflict in it, most times it does not receive awards or the most money.

People love mess, division, and hatred of all kinds. To fight and knock somebody out is the ultimate highlight of conversation. Believe it or not, it is even in the church. If the person did not get injured, there is great upset. Jesus' commandment was that we love one another (John 15:12). Because He loved us enough to die for our sins, we ought to love one another. This is also considered as being a peacemaker when you walk in peace, live in peace, and you are showing love. Please do not get it confused, to walk in love does not mean you love and look to get something back. That is not love. You love not wanting anything back. And, you do not get angry when you love and do not get anything back. Anger has no place in this. In fact, it is nowhere in the picture.

Controlling your anger in the heat of battle is not the easiest thing to do. In fact, it is the hardest thing to do. This is a popular subject that nobody wants to deal with. There was a time I was looking at an animal television show. There were two elephants getting into it with each other. One was a tad bit larger than the other one. While the other one really did not want the conflict the tad bit larger one was bringing, the larger one steadily came bucking and picking a fight with the tad bit smaller one, until a fight broke out. The point in sharing this short story is to show that you should try your hardest to shun from confusion and fighting. Unfortunately, the tab bit smaller one was defeated.

Keeping your cool and stay quiet in the heat of battle is one of the hardest things to do. The more you keep your cool, stay quiet and try to be patient with the person of conflict, the stronger they get. It would seem impossible to bring peace in the matter or to keep letting them know what is going on because they're yelling and carrying on. Nevertheless, you must remain patient and wait your turn to state your claim and pray for the other person or persons. If they are outrageously out of control and waiting for your turn seems impossible, walking away may be the best answer until they cool off and you two can peacefully come together with a calm conversation with the goal to resolve the conflict.

3

Open Rebuke is Good,
But Not With the Wrong Attitude

I was watching a talk show on television, which had different people on there talking about how they had been hurt within their relationships. One of them were a young man who was hurt by his dad not being in his life, which is the reason why he fathered over 30 kids by 50 different women. His mother happened to be on the show with him, as he stood and let her know that she hurt him as well. He shared in tears how she didn't love him and how she didn't show him how to treat a lady; which made him disrespect the women he was with and didn't care if he had fathered all of the kids, and didn't care about helping them take care of the children. The mother quickly cut him off as she stood up with an attitude and told him she wasn't loved

Open rebuke is open positive correction, without negative hidden motives.

either. She had issues herself. So that was her excuse. The point I am trying to make is that she made a true statement that could have possibly been received if she did not have the wrong attitude toward her son. She made what he was sharing with her as he poured his heart out to her seem unimportant. It turned the show completely into a Springer show and the purpose of uniting was lost. They argued and yelled back and forth. It was horrible.

When you are openly correcting a person or sharing your point, make sure that you come to them in a peaceful way without making them feel like their feelings and what they have shared is unimportant. The mother made her son feel as if she did not care whether or not he was hurt by her lack of love. And that it was not her fault that she did not love him as a result to him fathering all of those children and had sex with that many women. In relationships like these, it is helpful to know when to share the floor. Here's something to joint down:

1. Say what you have to say and allow the other person to share. Or, vice versa. Do not make them feel as if what they're sharing does not matter.
2. Listen to the person who is wounded, make them feel that you care about their hurt feelings, and if you are wrong, humble yourself and act like it and apologize.

3. Look for a conflict resolution—most times by apologizing and waiting on an opportunity to share how you feel and to say you're sorry. It can work both ways. Most times when you choose to listen, you will find that you were in error and the reality of the matter is the embarrassment of having to fix what you did or said wrong. It's harder when you're the guilty one, rather than the innocent one.

When I speak of open rebuking someone, I am speaking of open positive correction in love (Proverbs 27:5). Open rebuke is open positive correction, without negative hidden motives. I have found that you can change a person's entire life just by how you come at them and how you present yourself. You cannot rebuke a person if you are yelling just as they are. You cannot help calm a person down with cursing and outraged actions. Your rebuke must be solid with positive, calm words that have truth, love, correction, conviction, and change in them. I have personally witnessed this in my years of serving in the ministry and counseling others. They came yelling and thought it was the best way to express themselves as well as cursing, which made them feel better as to get their point across. However, the point wasn't good if a curse word wasn't with it. Although no one is perfect, you should work on their faults and struggles on a daily basis. We all have different struggles and we all have some type of dysfunctionalism about us. We are here on this earth together to be helpers one to another and not point out flaws in each other.

You may ask *"how do I open rebuke someone in love?"* I'll give you some points how below:

1. **Approach peacefully, carefully, and calmly:** Ask to talk to them in a peaceful way.
2. **Be honest and truthful:** After they agree, be honest by telling them how you feel in love.
3. **Get everything out in the open:** Do not hold anything back. After you have gotten everything out, let them have the floor to explain how they feel or to answer any questions, and so forth.
4. **Wait and listen to their response.**
5. **Close the conversation with a prayer of peace and for unity** (if received or the opportunity arises).

You may laugh at the points above, but they do work. You may also feel that they are too overboard or too hard to do. However, I want you to know that I have witnessed these points to be true. I have been in conflicts in which I did it my way with yelling and allowing the other person to get me worked up, and stormed out of the place of conflict. My way did not work so I had to make a change to better resolve conflicts within my life. Once you fail these points (tests), you'll have to repeat them until you pass them and become strong in these areas. It may not be with the same person, it may be with others or another conflict similar to the last one you went through.

You may not have a conversation with a person who may be willing to pray afterwards, but you can use your better judgment. The most important thing is to handle your relationships with care, and learn to be sensitive towards other's personality as you two or all work together to live in harmony and to keep a peaceful environment on a daily basis.

4

The Five Conflict Solutions

- *How to Resolve Church Conflicts*
- *How to Resolve Family Conflicts (mom, dad, siblings)*
- *How to Resolve Marital Conflicts*
- *How to Resolve Conflicts within Relationships*
- *How to Thrive Through Distraction to Avoid Conflicts*

How to Resolve Church Conflicts

Church conflicts are not new to this day and time. It swings way back to Biblical times when our Father, Jesus Christ was physically and actively here on earth. He set the standard on how to resolve conflict battles in the church. He would not allow anything to go on in the house of God that was not of Him. As we look in Matthew 21:12-13, Jesus was very angry with the church (temple) due to their negligence, greediness, selfishness, and actions of thieves. They were caught up in themselves rather than following the

> *Church conflict occur when there is lack of love, unity, and agreement.*

Will of the Father on how to conduct a church and its order. Instead, they promoted usury and Jesus casted them out in rage and let them know His *"house shall be called the house of prayer"*, although they *"made it a den of thieves."*

Church conflicts are resolved by the Word of God and not by evil actions that do not have any regards to the other person. I believe that Jesus was not only angry at the fact that they were promoting usury, but also at the fact that they did not want to be mindful of church order and God's promise of how we should act and operate in God's tabernacle.

One must be careful when operating in the church as it still belongs to the Father, and He still cares very much about them all. When disobedient, unethical actions are displayed in the church, it brings conflict that sometimes are not able to be handled. There are times when either person or persons, will leave the church or one or the other. There should not be a struggle of who is right or who is wrong, there should be a cohesive unit of Christian love and respect as each one follows the bylaws of the church's vision that God has given. Also, following what God has called each person to do, and sticking to that. There again, it is not what we want to do, or our great ideas of how we feel things should go, it is the Will of God and His plan for the church and the church's order that should prosper week after week.

Church conflicts occur when there is lack of love, unity, and agreement. You must understand that getting along does not only revolves around you, it also revolves around everyone who is present and in that particular ministry in the church. There are no little "I's" and "big Me's". Everyone is responsible for his or her own actions and attitude. Everyone is on the same level of responsibility, accountability and is expected to operate in a Christ-like manner at all times.

Although the sinful natures of our flesh at times get in the way, repentance and forgiveness must quickly follow as soon as possible. If an unbeliever or a wounded Christian comes to worship service, he or she should see your fruits and display of who, what, and how a Christian should act. They should not leave there wondering if you were saved or not.

The book of Acts specifically focuses on the early church and the spread of the gospel (Discipleship/Apostleship) immediately after the resurrection of Jesus Christ. There was much persecution and conflict against the Christians and the Apostles. Church conflicts were then and they still are now.

Nowadays church conflicts are just like regular conflicts in relationships or families. Most Christian Believers really do not care about what other Christian Believers in the church think or say. They are mean and controlling wanting everything their way.

When there are conflicts within workers in the church: the clergy, deacons, deaconess, first lady, the men and women's ministry, singles, children, youth, young adults, the board, administration, chair financial committee members, and so on, there is conflict in the entire church. When there is division there, it falls on the entire church body and administration. To resolve these types of situations, each member who is involved, should go to the throne of God instead of trying to handle them on your own and create worse problems. It is important to go to the head leader (pastor or delegate) and talk about the conflict, pray about it together, and leave it in the office.

The Christian Believer should strive for peace at all times. When there was conflict within the people of God, they came together and prayed to get an answer from God instead of hashing it out and tearing up the church (Acts 6:1-7).

Whenever your peace seems to be violated, quickly run to God in prayer and let Him handle the situation at hand. You can never go wrong allowing the Holy Spirit to minister to the matter. Many times, we as Christians try to handle our own problems on our own, when at most times they are much too great to handle. So, why not put them in the hands of the Lord? He is true to His Word in working every problem out for you whether as an individual, within your ministry, within your church, within the administration (behind the scenes), within the leadership committee, or any other. To be a peacemaker, exemplifying peace has to happen for every part of the Believer. It not only should work for you as an individual, but it should work for the entire ministry, cohesively as a whole.

Workshops, seminars, conferences, prayer revivals, meetings, and an entire church fast are good when there is conflict within the church or ministry. It is the plan of the devil to bring division and confusion among the Saints of God so that God's perfect, divine, unified plan cannot be fulfilled. He works hard to work in the minds and hearts of the members to operate against each other to bring fighting, bickering, jealousy, pride, hatred, and other promiscuous sins in hopes to tear the members a part so they will stop coming and if they stop coming, the church will suffer and eventually shut down and may even close up. This should not be so. Every member is responsible for his or her own actions. It is important to stay close to the Vine of Jesus Christ. How do you stay close to the Vine in order to keep peace and operate in love at all cost? My answer is below:

1. **Get in God's presence.** Spend time with God through prayer and supplication on a daily basis.

2. **Read your Bible constantly.** I am not saying to be religious, but read it with an open heart, mind, Spirit, and soul. Do not read it like you're perfect and have no flaws. As you read, constantly look in your mirror, reflect on your own self and life. This will help you to be real and honest and your healing and deliverance will come quicker. If every member accomplishes this, it will be a peaceful ministry. Everyone will be unified, and miracles will happen right before your eyes.

3. **Make prayer and fasting your way of life.** The Word of God says some thing's come only by *"prayer and fasting"* (Matthew 17:21). Prayer and fasting will break chains, strongholds, and bring change that not only just praying alone will do.

Successful Peacemaking Comes When You Value
Your Leader, Those You Serve With,
& Those Around You—Keeps Away Conflict.

I have experienced while serving in ministry members who did not value the leader. They valued visiting pastors and leaders who came to speak at the church for a particular service, workshops, conferences, or revival services. However, they did not value the presiding leading pastor or leaders serving at their own local church. For example, they spoke highly of the visiting speakers—pastors or leaders, saying how they spoke so well and learned so much. They snickered questions of why the pastor and leaders couldn't speak like they did. When the event was well over with, they were still talking about how they learned so much by listening to their sermons and all the literature they provided in the particular service, workshops, conferences, and/or revival services. On the other hand, with the presiding pastor, elder, or leader(s) leading in ministry, their conversations were never satisfied. They always complained about something he or she said, or their unimportant opinions, which served of no value of how the visiting pastor(s) could preach or teach better than he could or she could; and everything that was wrong in the church. They did not value the leader, the ministry leaders, or the church. When you value your leader, you speak highly of them. You look to learn something new from them. You follow their vision with excitement and eagerness to help serve and expand the vision for the kingdom.

When you value your leader, you are ready to hear what they have to say. What they said stays with you and when you get home, it still lingers within you as you pull out all the notes and rehearse it as if it was the first time you heard it. You cannot judge a book by its cover. Never go by what they look like or sound like on the outside. Most times, you will be wrong and have to go back and repent.

Let me give you a couple of keys on how to value your leader and to keep away conflict:

1. Do not judge him or her. Do not look for every single solitary thing that you see wrong with them. No one is perfect. Most times, you will see negative flaws especially if you look for them.

2. Speak highly of him or her. Valuing your leader and those you serve in ministry with, runs deep and most times when you value, you regard him or her as of importance. Your focus should be only on the message of what they are sent by God to give you.

3. Do not make preconceptions. Do not assume.

When you do not assume, you can learn a lot because you're open to receive, rather than close yourself up to look for what is wrong, or anticipate that you will not receive from them.

There was a certain minister at a church I served at years ago. When it was his time to preach the Word of God, nobody wanted to listen because his sermons were so dry and boring. When he came up to the podium to speak, everybody literally sunk in their seats. And, I was right with them. But on this particular Sunday, what I perceived to happen, did not. His sermon was more powerful than most well-known speakers I'd ever heard on television. I took so many notes, almost running out of writing room. I valued what he had to say, and not prejudged him, and it helped. Whereas, before I prejudged, assuming that his sermon would be boring and non-effective for me. I was wrong. So I share that to say that this has helped me not to prejudge and to wait and receive each speaker or person as they are at that given moment.

Do not judge by what others say or how they look. This is also for personal relationships you encounter on a daily basis. In addition, certainly do not judge them by their mannerisms. Do not prejudge their stances, gestures or movements. Your focus should be on the message with an open mind, and ready to receive something that you need and can change your life forever.

How to Resolve Family Conflicts
(mom, dad, siblings, uncle, aunt, cousins, etc.)

Dealing with other people is hard enough at times, but dealing with something more familiar like the family is much more challenging. I have encountered witnessing many family conflicts and ordeals. One of which I can remember was between my brothers who were teenagers at the time. They were just horsing around, playing boxing with the new boxing gloves our mom had just bought for them.

Just as they were punching each other, the game became more serious and one of them took a wild punch in the stomach. He got mad and they started taunting and tussling each other. Peace was nowhere to be found. They were both fighting and yelling at one another as my mom came and broke them up with a good lashing and took the gloves from them. At that moment, no one would dare mention Jesus Christ as the answer, and the pure fact that we must all get along. Those two were not hearing that. However, it would have been true. There are many more family conflicts in which are much more heated than that one. However, when there is conflict among the family, it is encouraged that they all come together and find a resolution to the problem, great or small, that is making them fight. When you think about it, none of us will be on this earth forever, and time is precious with your family, friendships, and relationships. Make the best out of what you have and make it your goal to get along and try your best to be the best peacemaker you can.

The answer to family conflict is what Jesus Christ in Mark 12:31 had to say about everyone loving one another. He said to love your neighbor (each other) as you love yourself. This means at all cost. I realize that it is hard to love at all times due to challenging moments that may arise. However, just as they arise, you must resort back to what Jesus said, "love". I had to do this in a conflict I had with a friend in the past. The argument wanted to escalate but I quickly got quiet remembering what the Word of God said about "love", and the argument was left with silence and quick apologies. Trust me, it is quite challenging, but it can be done. It has to be done, or you will stay in heated battles or small conflicts that will escalate to heated battles with not so good endings. As I have stated earlier, conflict is everywhere. No one can run from potential conflict but we can learn from our mistakes and run from those that try to rise up in the future.

How to Resolve Marital Conflict

Marriage is sacred to God as it should be to both parties involved. Just as you two wholeheartedly repeated those sacred and lawful vows to one another, you two should wholeheartedly live and keep those vows with one another.

Seeing each other on a daily basis can become quite challenging especially when conflict or disagreement rises. Most marriages end as a result of divorce because of the inability to compromise, work together, money problems, and unfaithfulness. Although it is true that you will not agree on everything, it is encouraged that when you do not agree, just agree to disagree. What I mean by this is, respect your spouse's opinion or the way they feel, and keep it moving. Do not harp on the same ol' things. Do not try to control their opinions, answers, or decisions. When you do not do this, this is being a peacemaker in times of disagreement. This is how you resolve conflict within your marriage. It takes two to argue. No one can argue by themselves. If you see someone attempt this, he or she would look mighty funny and weird.

Praying together as a couple is the most important tool to resolving conflict as it arise between you two. The Word of God speaks that we should all *"pray without ceasing"* (1 Thessalonians 5:17). This is true as crises may come up. Because the marriage is rooted and grounded in prayer, it will break yokes and chains of confusion and make it easier to see the answer on how to resolve the situation at hand. Whereas, it is very hard to see when prayer has not been the center for the marriage. The door was left open for the devil to come in and operate, bring in division, confusion, constant fighting back and forth (mental, verbal, and physical abuse), and even infidelity. For more study on this topic, read my book "Winning Together".

How to Resolve Conflicts within Relationships

Relationship battles can last for a while, as most never fully unite back together. Most relationship battles normally start from simple, silly things that could have been avoided in the beginning. The norm happens, "you always wanna' be right," "you think you know it all," "I can't stand you," "You always want the last word," "you always want things your way." These are the types of phrases that are said in the heat of an argument. It takes a lot of work making any relationship work on a daily basis, this is why you must put your best foot forward and strive to be the best peacemaker as much as possible.

In relational battles, forgiveness must be the center. I have never seen a perfect disagreement. Most disagreements turn out very ugly and feelings get hurt to a degree that one of the parties leave in a rage of anger and unforgiveness.

True forgiveness and love must be practiced to resolve conflicts within relationships. You can say you forgive that person or persons, but in your heart you hate them. Believe you me, it will show whether or not you mean what you say. True forgiveness shows in the way you treat a person. It shows in your actions and attitude. If you are operating the opposite of true forgiveness, you should say to yourself constantly, "I will choose to treat everybody right today." "I will choose to forgive today." You should refuse to get an attitude about everything. You will find that when you make this conscious decision to change and confess this daily, more people will choose to be around you. The Word of God says if you want a friend, you must first show yourself friendly (Proverbs 18:24). Being friendly to everyone rebukes any chance for conflicts and disagreements to come in. Jesus made every effort for His people to find peace in the mist of every disagreement. The book of Acts is full of disagreement and confusion. It is based on truth and lies. It is based on forgiveness and unforgiveness. Paul, once known as Saul, is a perfect example of his conversion from a Christian hater to a God and Christian lover (Acts 9). He ends up being one of the most counted on Apostles that Jesus Christ could have ever used. The disciples traveled compelling, just as Jesus did, compelling the people to believe in God and be baptized in the Holy Ghost (Spirit) as there was much controversy with that. Many of the disciples had to forgive for the persecutions they faced. So we see that conflict, disagreement, and confusion did not just begin in this day and time. This began centuries ago. However, the answer to resolve it is to go to Jesus and remember His covenant of what He says about loving one another as yourself (1 Thessalonians 4:9), loving your enemies (Matthew 5:44), esteeming one another higher than yourself (1 Thessalonians 5:11-13), do to others as you would have them do to you. Our God is our mediator and He is our Prince of Peace. He comes to bring peace in every situation and dispute. He helps us when we cannot help ourselves. He comes to bring agreement and peace when heated disputes are way out of control. God is in the mist of reconciliation. He can mend anything that has been broken and torn apart. He is the

Mender of broken hearts. If your heart has ever been broken and you have been badly bruised, He can mend your scars and wounds. He can reconcile you back together. He can bring those person or persons back in your life and mend what the devil meant to tear apart, back together as if it was never torn apart. He specializes in this. He is perfect in this. He never fails.

Pick Up the Broken Glass Pieces

Within every antagonizing disagreement, there are emotional scars and wounds, broken feelings, disappointments, failures, guilt, and suicidal thoughts that are shattered all over the place. They have come as distractions. Most are small pieces in which have turned into large pieces because the two involved did not resolve the conflict, or did not do it quick enough. They allowed it to escalate and more pieces fell and shattered until they all piled up on top of each other to a point where you or they exploded. You cannot live in the past nor can you thrive on being phony or hypocritical just to keep peace, but all the while, either burning up inside or is hurting inside. I encourage you to pick up the broken pieces in your life, quietly and peacefully talk about what it is that is bothering you, or what you are hurting about to the person who has hurt you or has made you angry, and move on. The devil wants you to hold all of that hurt, anger, and pain on the inside and never get it out. Some have even taken this to their grave. Do not allow the devil to defeat you nor your relationship(s). Pick up the broken pieces if you have to do it one by one until you get it all out and release them all. Then move on by not bringing it or them back up, slamming it or them in their faces again and again, holding up a shield of defense and shutting down and shutting yourself out, or closing yourself up in a closet or a box. Mistakes happen, whether it is you as the guilty person or as the victim, we all have had our share of mistakes and letdowns. Now pick yourself up and move on by canceling conflict completely out of your life and relationship. I say to you now, by the strips of Jesus Christ you are healed (Isaiah 53:4-5).

How to Thrive Through Distraction to Avoid Conflict

Being a great ignorer is a great way to thrive through distraction to avoid conflict. There was a time when I was concentrating on finishing a task that I had started that had an immediate deadline. I was pressed for time and no time to even sit down. All of a sudden distraction came knocking at the door. An unexpected visitor showed up to visit. I could not turn them away so I thought I could entertain them for a minute and maybe they would get the hint that I was very busy and needed time to myself. Nope. Didn't work. They ended up staying all night and the task was not completed but was terminated. I was very angry and did my best to avoid conflict. Distraction is a set up to cancel an assignment. It comes to stop and to hinder agreement. It comes to shut the door on any potential blessing.

Most times the person hides to keep from dealing with distraction. Therefore making conflict worse than what it could have been had it been handled up front. The more you hide, the more the other person strives to make you mad or madder by distracting you more and more in order to bring discord. At this point, you should continue to be silent and seek to leave the scene before something more serious comes out of it than expected. You are not required to stay in torment or discomfort as you are being picked on in their presence. You can flee the scene and let God deal with them. 1 Corinthians 10:13 says when temptations rise in your face, God will provide you a way of escape. He will allow you to escape confusion and move you to a more comfortable place of peace.

When you can be the bigger person by not entertaining mess, you are thriving through distraction and avoiding conflict.

5

What Do You Do When the Dark Smoke of Conflict Clears?

Just as I have stated in my last chapter, you can flee the scene that is filled with gun smoke. Just take off running as fast as you can. But it is a challenge to flee the scene that is filled with anger, rage, torment, bullying, picking, jealousy, hatred, and strife.

Jesus Christ is the most courageous of us all. It took courage for Him to come as Himself down on this earth to take on all of the

Do not allow people to have power over you with the negative things they say to you.

sins of the world in order that sinners would have a chance to eternal life. He went through the dark smoke of conflict, brutal beatings, hatred, and pain but was still strong in standing His ground for what was right. And He was also innocent. He never did anything wrong. So, as you are going through your tough times of persecution, disagreement, and conflict with those who are a challenge to get along with, remember Jesus, Who died for the very thing that you are having a hard time getting through. As Jesus was able to get the victory over all of His haters, persecutors, and those who did not want Him to be right, you can too because He set the standard for you to do so. I realize that is easier said than done. However, as it is exercised enough, it will become easier the more you practice it when or if those times should arise. As we look in John 18:10-11, we can clearly see that Jesus was the greatest peacemaker there was and still is today through His Holy Spirit.

When the officers came with torches and weapons to take Him away, He already knew what they wanted and knew that it was something that He had to go through because of the purpose for which He was sent. Peter on the other hand, not thinking about the purpose but looking at the conflicted battle before him, and the fact that they were bullying the One he looked out for at the time, took out his sword and proceeded to cut off the ear of the officer. Jesus quick in the peace making Spirit, quickly and aggressively said to Peter, *"Put up thy sword into the sheath: the cup which my Father hath given me, shall I not drink it?"* This proves that in the mist of the most heated battle of their lives, Jesus did not stoop to the enemy's level. He remained calm and was not quick to respond (James 1:19). In this same way, you have to follow this same example and take the initiative not to lose your temper and become vulnerable to those who want to see you lose it, and want you to bow down to their level. They strive to have power over you. They were actually sent on an assignment from the enemy take away your peace, make you unhappy, to distract you, to take you out, to embarrass you, to hurt and to pick on you, and even to stop your God sent purpose. Do not allow people to have power over you with the negative things they say to you. Show that you are a peacemaker and shun from them as you keep your joy—smile as you walk away with a victorious attitude—refusing to entertain wrong.

6

What Do You Do After the Dark Smoke of Conflict Clears and It's Your Fault?

It is easy to handle a heated conflict when it is not your fault, however, in a situation when it is your fault, it comes as a convicting and humbling experience.

Most times when people are unhappy with themselves, they will try to make others unhappy. They know that they are wrong while doing it but do not want you to tell them they are. So, things blow up, and they are happy because they got what they wanted; and they soon leave the scene without being apologetic nor caring about all the wounds and brutal scars they just created. I have learned that these types of people are being controlled by haunted pasts, hidden agendas, and unhappy encounters. I have also found that there are some who are the opposite but

> *Most times when people are unhappy with themselves, they will try to make others unhappy.*

still considered guilty. They are unhappy themselves, but wish someone would help them on the inside, but they don't know how to ask for help. Instead, they make others unhappy by their disruptive actions, negative words, attitudes, approaches, outlooks, and inability to jell with others. If you are guilty of these such actions, after the smoke clears, you have to humble yourself by being honest with yourself, repent to God and go to that person(s) and tell them that you are sorry, and ask them if they would forgive you. You must seek yourself to much prayer and counseling. You must begin to find something good about your life and about yourself. If we all really try, we can all find something, if not several unhappy things about ourselves, circumstances, and life. But to focus on the good will always make you feel better and will be healthier for you. Unhappiness carries pain, sickness, and depression. However, happiness carries love, joy, and peace of mind within.

Remove condemnation. Remove the guilt and blame you are carrying from things you hate you did in your past. The Holy Spirit convicts us when we have done wrong, but thank God He does not constantly remind us and make us feel bad everyday of our lives about them (Romans 8:1).

Make a goal everyday of your life that you are going to walk in peace and have peace with all men on this earth. I was reading in the Bible in Romans 7:15-23, where it talks about *"wanting to do right, but evil is always present."* Or try this one, *"What I do I do not understand because I am not doing what I would like to, but I am doing the very thing I hate."* The enemy wants you to lose in your relationships and with acquaintances you are around, or you come in contact with on a daily basis. He does not want you to have peace with all men. However, on the inside of you, you have this feeling of you just want to do right and to treat everybody right without having a disagreement. This is what this passage of scripture is talking about. You want to do the right thing and get along with your spouse, kids, supervisor, coworker, teacher, friend(s), or the person in the grocery store, but somehow evil always show up and there is always a heated battle or fusing match back and forth. This is the devil who comes in as a thief to steal and rob the love and peace between you two (John 10:10). You have to stop his plan. You have to say to yourself that you refuse to allow the devil to rob you and your relationship's peace and love for one another anymore. And let it be just that. Strive to be a peacemaker as you let them have the floor by listening to them, loving them no matter what, and by being wise—knowing when to talk and when to be quiet.

Dust Yourself Off

If you can imagine a haze of smoke after it has almost cleared the room, it has this unclear slightly smoky residue in which rests over the atmosphere, you can imagine your life and current aftermath of failure from your most heated conflict. You can see, but there is still some debris and residue left. That is the area that you should deal with concerning dusting yourself off.

Take a car that spins off with a pile of sand underneath as you stand right behind it. It, at first is very dusty and smoky and as time past, it finally goes back to normal. But if you notice one thing, your clothes and your body are covered with dust from the sand and debris. That is the area where I am talking about dusting off. The smoke of conflict is over whether in your relationship, marriage, friendship, with the kids, with your siblings, church ministry, on your job, with a coworker, in the grocery store, out on the streets, in your local whatever. It is over, and now you have made the mistake and hopefully you have repented and asked God to forgive you. It is time to move on. Many times people do not move on. They do not dust themselves off. They keep right on battling. They have to make sure the other party has gotten what they deserve, and I'm not talking about winning a prize. They have made every point to give them a piece of their mind, and are not sorry for what they have said, done, or the damage they have made. This is not dusting yourself off. Dusting yourself off means to completely choose to do whatever takes to bring peace in the matter, and then afterwards leave it alone.

Below are a couple of points on how to shake the dust from your clothes in the most heated battles:

1. Choose to be the bigger person and apologize or do whatever it takes to bring peace in the argument and/or disagreement.
2. Get quiet and wait for the other one to respond.
3. Keep reminding yourself that it is not worth the fight.
4. Go back to what the Word of God says about loving each other no matter what.
5. Rest until the smoke clears and the conflict fades away.

It is not always easy to win in every conflicted battle. However, it is essential to strive to win as much as you can and be the peacemaker that God is calling you to be everyday of your life.

7

Confrontation is the Key to a Healthy Relationship

- ❖ Approach confrontation unselfishly
- ❖ Do not draw back when emotions arise during confrontation
- ❖ Run to confront immediately without waiting
- ❖ Listen before you speak is where you win
- ❖ 1/4 percent you, 1/3 percent them
- ❖ Seek to understand rather than to agree
- ❖ Seek a plan of action

Confrontation is the key to an unhealthy relationship. Most people run from confrontation. Either they shove it off on someone else to handle, or they try to forget it ever happened, or they run and hide until the smoke would somehow clear. In most cases, the

Confrontation is healthy when in a relationship that both parties are willing to approach it the right way.

smoke is the last thing to clear. It usually escalates until you are forced to confront the issue at hand anyway. I can recall numerous of times when I had to confront a situation and did not want to. I am guilty on both ends. I was guilty as I tried to run from confronting the situation, and was also guilty in trying to confront the situation. I did not want to deal with the hassle of possible confusion and a potential argument that I was not ready for. I was also guilty from confronting a situation that I handled wrong by confronting it the wrong way. You can only win in confrontation when you approach it the right way. Confrontation is healthy when in a relationship that both parties are willing to approach it the right way.

Below are some factors that I have seen when people have approached a confrontation the wrong way:

- *Sent someone else to do it.* They never showed up to confront the person, they sent someone else to do it.
- *Unplugged the phone.* They totally disconnected themselves from them to keep from dealing with the issue(s).
- *Played the blame game.* No one took the blame or opened themselves up for potentially being wrong. They assumed that the other person was guilty and drilled blame into them.
- *A heated battle.* Lashing back and forth bringing up 30 years of past faults, shames, and guilt's.

- *Had a physical boxing match.* Each person or persons involved never positively confronted verbally, they felt that hashing it out physically was the best method.

Most times when you confront a person, they will have an emotional reaction to what you said. Unfortunately, their emotional reaction may fall in the category of the bullets above. The goal here is to approach the confrontation <u>the right way</u> so that you both or you all can win in the battle of the confrontation, like below:

- *Handle it yourself.* Do not send others to do your job to confront the person(s). They don't know the conflict you and them are having. It is not their business anyway unless they are involved.
- *Make sure all of your lines of communication is open.* Do not unplug your phone or look at the caller ID and not answer it. We tend to do this with telemarketers, but this should not be done with that person or those you need to find a resolution with.
- *Blame yourself first.* You should go into the confrontation blaming yourself first. See what it is that you may have done to cause such actions attitudes or the negative situation. Sometime it may be something you may have done or said that may have sparked the

conflict and do not realize it. I have been guilty of this before.

- *Never resort to a heated battle.* This will never resolve the conflict. You confronting the issue by going 30 years back bringing up what they did or said does not resolve the conflict. It is only resolved by dealing with the matter at hand. Handling what's right in front of you at that moment.

- *Erase the physical fight.* You shooting your guns back and forth until a man goes down first never resolves the conflict. It only escalates into something more deadly like years of jail time, or life threatening injuries, or even you or them resting in a coffin.

The key is to win in confrontation, not to lose. If this is not your goal, you should not confront at all. The bullets above list positive ways to confront and to handle confrontation. Nobody's saying they are perfect ways, but in most cases they work if approached right.

Approach Confrontation Unselfishly

There was a time I had a confrontation with one of my siblings. We argued what seemed like forever about how each other felt in the matter. As we verbally lashed back and forth about what we, ourselves were not happy with, when it was all over with, we realized we never heard each other's side or how that person really felt. I find it very easy to get caught up in hearing what yourself has to say while shouting to the top of your lungs over the other person(s), while never hearing what they have to say. I have also seen where one of the persons involved, listened just a tenth of a second as the other person only got to make a half of a sentence of explaining what was bothering them before the other person involved, cut in and started yelling. They never stopped until they completely took control of the conflict and have made themselves the victim.

Your approach to confrontation should be "how can I make things right between us?" "I'm sorry and I'm willing to try to make things right between us." Can you do this? Does this work for you?

Going into a conflict with an, I could careless attitude will make you miserable for the rest of your life. The world is full of those kinds of people. This is why they can cut you off on the road and never apologize. Actually blow at you as if you did them wrong. You should care how you treat others. You should care how you come off when around other people. You should always be careful in choosing your words while speaking to others. You should feel some type of way when you may have hurt another person's feelings, instead of knowing what you did and not caring one way or another to apologize and get it right with them. This is a peacemaker—you look for a chance to bring peace in the matter rather than chaos.

Approaching a matter unselfishly is to listen and see how they feel first. Find out what is bothering them first, if the person has come to you with an issue. If you are the person with the issue, unselfishly make a remark of, "I realize that I am the one with the issue and I'm sorry."

Do not Drawback When Emotions Arise During Confrontation

While counseling a married couple, the wife began sharing how she felt about her husband's negative attitude around the house. She became emotional and he drew back and over powered her without taking notice of how she felt. He cut her off and strongly stated his claim on what she said.

As I counseled a mother and her son, the mother began stating how she was fed up with her son's ways and she couldn't take his lazy bad attitude anymore. The son quickly shut down and drew back into a reverse mode of quietness. I tried talking to him and he would not respond. So I asked the mother to leave the room while I spoke to him alone. Once she left the room, he began to open up and share how he felt, which wasn't nearly how she felt.

I share these real life examples to say that it is important not to shut down when the other person(s) is sharing how they feel about the conflict you two or them are having. Drawing back can destroy the entire goal to bring peace in the matter and move on to try to better the relationship or situation.

Crying while sharing is not drawing back. There is a difference. You draw back when you shut down, get quiet and stay quiet as you refuse to talk, do not want to deal with the conflict, close your mouth with nothing to say, or leave the scene unresolved. Sometimes you have to cry in order to release the hurt. However, crying should not be used as a means to make the other person feel bad or bring guilt upon them. If you began to cry while releasing the hurt as you say how you feel in a receivable way, it can be received by the other person. Unlike crying to make them draw back and shut down to make them feel bad. This is not a peacemaking resolution, it is a control mechanism.

Run to Confront Immediately Without Waiting

Most people have the tendency to run from confrontation, rather than to confrontation. They do not want to deal with it one way or the other. While I have seen some run to confrontation, ready to correct rather than confront with the goal to come into agreement and settle out in peace. Very little are like this. They do not care or are too afraid. You should not be afraid to confront the other person. The problem comes when confrontation is confronted in a negative way. If approached the right way, it will strengthen the relationship, strengthen the matter at hand, bring understanding and resolution; and leave with quick relief.

When you wait to confront the other person(s), it only makes the matter worse. Things worsen, open doors of lies come in from outside parties that don't have anything to do with the issue you two are having, and unforgiveness festers to deep inner iniquity of anger, resentment, hatred, sickness in your body, feelings of retaliation, and escalation of bringing in others in the conflict to help you retaliate and embarrass them.

Inner iniquity can bring sickness in your body. Keeping things inside without ever confronting them and venting them, can bring sicknesses like painful migraine headaches, feeling of faintness, dizziness, heart palpitations, nervous breakdowns, high blood pressure, heart attack, stroke, cancer, suicide, and so on. While no one wants to experience these things, the resolution is to confront the matter in a peacemaking positive way. If this is still too sensitive for you, go and talk (vent) to someone you can trust who will not make things worse and maybe can be a positive third party in the matter only if the other person agrees.

Listen Before you Speak is Where you Win

I have heard this scripture, *"be quick to listen, and slow to speak"* (James 1:19). I find it to be true. I have been guilty of this as I spoke out before listening to the other person and had the entire conflict wrong. It wasn't the way it was, as I thought. Had I listened to that person before speaking, I would have found out that I interpreted the situation completely wrong.

Everybody wants to be heard. I have seen in cases where one person have talked and talked and talked and did not listen to the other person and the conflict became worse. Whereas, in other situations I have seen where one person made it their point to listen to them entirely until they gave them the floor. I found this method to be more rewarding and they both won the conflict that day. The two persons had a chance to vent out their feelings entirely and felt so much better afterwards. It can be a bit challenging to listen to the other person entirely, especially if they say something you do not agree with. In this case you should write down what you do not agree with while they are talking until they are completely finished, and then you can expound on those things said that you did not agree with or need more clarity on when it's your time to share. It should be a give and take situation between both persons. This works. I have tried it myself and found that it does work. I'll admit, it's not easy, but it is doable. Without these types of resolutions, things would stay out of whack and we would all live in constant confusion.

When you listen instead of talking too much, especially while the other person is talking, you will find you may be the guilty one at fault. When you are wrong, it is certainly a reality, self-check. If you are not wrong and are yelling over them, it makes you look wrong and out of control. Controlling yourself while having self-discipline and stability within, is key when listening until it is your time to state your claim in the matter.

1/4 Percent You, 1/3 Percent Them

When going into conflict, it should be less of you as much as possible. You should never totally control the conversation while never giving the other person a chance to state their claim of how they feel—making your words the final answer. 1/4 percent should belong to you, and a 1/3 percent should belong to them. This is how peacemaking resolution should be your focal point to bringing peace within the conflict.

Seek to Understand Rather Than to Agree

You may never agree with each other, so seek to understand how the other person feels and move on from there, while holding no grudges, animosity, or unforgiveness.

80 percent of the time, common conflicts do not result in agreement. The hindrance here is, understanding is not the center of focus. You're too busy trying to agree instead of listening and understanding how the other person feels. Agree to disagree. You may never agree with the other person, however, understand that they have a right to feel the way they feel, right or wrong, you cannot change that. So, understanding is the only thing left if you two want to come out on top as winners in the matter.

Seek a Plan of Action

Two people can argue all night. I have seen some in-laws argue all night until they got tired and the yelling eventually stopped and resumed the next day. The same argument was brought back up weeks later with the same intense yelling as they did the first time they started fighting. What I realized is there was no plan of action. They two did not sit down and first listen to each other, nor did they seek to better the conflict for the future so that recapping, reliving, and reviving the past would come up weeks later. They did not write down better ways on how to handle where they two were failing with getting along. They two did not propose what they were going to work on themselves instead of blaming the other one and threatening them to change or else.

A plan of action is to take authority of the conflict by actively turning it around to a positive outcome. Here's some ideas:

- Be quick to listen and slow to speak.
- Understand how the other person feels and respect how they feel. Do not try to control or change the way they feel because it's not what you agree with, however, it is how they feel and you should respect that even if you do not agree.
- You two can write down your faults and what you are doing to offend the other person, pray together, and actively practice not doing those things mentioned on paper.
- Give each other some time to breath and release their feelings. Come back together and start over again but this time take precaution not to do or say those things you know will offend the other person again. It should not be your goal to go over the same old things and the same old arguments and disagreements everyday. It should be your goal to see how each other feels, take precaution by not saying or doing those things and move on. Key word "move on."

8

Discipline Comes from Much Discipline

In order to obtain discipline, you would have had to be disciplined yourself. I can recall as a child, my mother was a disciplinary. When she told us to do something and we did not do it, we were disciplined right away and that was that. She did not allow us to run over her and say all manner of evil to her and get away with it. As a result, we as adults today appreciate her discipline although we didn't then. We are now disciplined adults

> *In order to obtain discipline, you would have had to be disciplined yourself.*

ourselves who teach our children the same way we were taught. If you notice that the word "discipline" is a long word for disciple? The disciples in the Bible who followed Jesus were very disciplined. Jesus taught them well in the book of Matthew, Mark, Luke, and John. He did not take no stuff. What I like about the disciples was that they not only were disciplined by Jesus, but they also made a conscious decision to live and to do right by all people. After you have been taught and have received discipline, you now know how to walk right, act right, treat others right, and always do the right thing and make right choices. You are considered well-disciplined now. You're not going to run in and out of jail, constantly getting in trouble, not having any control over your mouth, or being a busy body (in everybody's business).

Being disciplined does not feel good. In fact, after it is over, you think about the consequences, and strive not to ever go that route or make that same mistake again because you do not want to experience that scolding again. It is the same with God. He disciplines those He love (Revelation 3:19). If He did not, you would not have self-control as His child and would do what you want to do without remorse or feeling.

9

Peacemaking through Forgiveness

Forgiveness is one of the hardest things to do after you have been hurt and wounded. It is the last word you want to hear especially when it first happens.

Peacemaking through forgiveness is encouraged as you make peace with the person you have wronged and want to get it right with them. Paul is a great example in the book of Acts. Before he was converted, he hated Christians and persecuted them to a great degree. However, after Christ saved him and changed his life, he became one of the most powerful men in ministry in those times. He would go out and minister from town to town, compelling men, women, boys, and girls to come to Christ. They knew his past, which made it very difficult for him to convince them to turn and to follow Christ. The point I am trying to make here is that Paul had a very bad

> *Peacemaking through forgiveness is encouraged as you make peace with the person you have wronged and want to get it right with them.*

past and needed the people to forgive him. If you look at it, it is very hard to forgive someone who have encouraged someone to have you beat up or have you killed. God is calling us to forgive one another as many times as it takes in order to keep your slat clean and also to keep peace as much as possible.

Peter, one of the disciples asked Jesus how many times are we to forgive one another in Matthew 18:21-22. Jesus answered, "…until seventy times seven." So if Christ says we should forgive this many times, you have to strive to match this scripture in your own life everyday. I realize that it is hard because I have been deeply hurt and wounded before in my life, and it is very hard to forgive someone who have wronged you either through words or actions. But what helps you to heal and to forgive is to think of a time when you wronged or wounded someone, either by words or actions. Remember what you felt like after you did it and you knew you were wrong? How you wanted them so badly to forgive you? Well, this is how you have to think when it comes to you on the receiving end (the forgiver) instead of the giving end (the one needing forgiveness).

Jesus was the greatest example of forgiving those who persecuted Him and beat Him imaginably. We could never go through the suffering and the torture that He went through and come out of it alive, let alone to be set in a place to forgive.

86

But guess what, He did. And He still does today as He forgives our sins on a daily basis. I know you may be saying, "you're way too deep." And I would come back by saying, "I'm not deep enough." We are sent to this earth to follow after the things of righteousness and after Jesus Christ's examples of how to treat people and how we should talk to one another. As you strive after these things, daily, you will be victorious in this area of being a peacemaker ready to forgive your brethren if he or she does you wrong.

10

The Peacemaking Ministry

It is very challenging to have a peacemaking ministry in this world today. However, God has held us accountable to come as close as possible. He has made it as accessible as possible for us to get along. He has provided the Biblical preaching and teaching word, counseling through the ministry, books based on the Word of God that cater to your need, and CD and DVD ministries.

Conflict will come, but it is how you handle it when it does.

With every ministry, there is potential conflict somewhere at any given point and time. While no one encourages it, it is prevalent and the door can swing open at any moment. Conflicts come in the form of all sorts of people, things, and ways. Most are very petty which the enemy has conjured up anyway. He loves confusion so he seeks who is weak at that very moment that he can use to do it. As I have stated before, this is when there has to be constant areas available in the ministry to step in before these areas of attack can manifest, and cancel the assignment of conflicts that seek to devour the Saints of God, the church body, the administration, the ministerial staff, the clergy, the pastor, the deacon and/or deaconess board, the youths, the children, at the school, the staff on your job, and so on. You must encourage the church to be a peacemaking church. You must encourage your job to be a peace making job. You must encourage your school and peers at the school to be a peacemaking school and peers.

Nowadays when we think of the church, we think of sinful misleading pastors who have messed up, or what fight went down, or she had the nerve to call me out of my name and then turned and called the other lady sister. It is to no surprise when a church closes its doors due to bickering and fighting. There is more fighting going on in the church than outside. In my book "Church Hurt", I speak more on this type of subject. Christ's Name has stepped out of people's mouths when in conversation about the church. Certainly, I am not speaking of every church, but I am speaking of most. And, certainly I realize there is no perfect church either, but if you want a peacemaking, Christ filled church, it must function like it each time the doors are open.

The Word of God has to be put into practice when dealing with one another while operating in ministry. It is not about what you think, it is about what did God say or what He thinks. Many times the church ministry falls short when everybody feels that their opinion is what God says, when in fact none of us have the right or the position to speak as if we are God. If you are doing this, you are operating in a very dangerous spirit. God built the church on order in the Old Testament and that is the same order that He requires today. We must be holy, clean from sin, forsaking not the assembly of ourselves, worship together, treating one another in brotherly love, esteeming one another higher than yourself, greeting each other with a holy kiss and hug, coming together and working together as you agree to disagree, and realizing that they may not go with your idea. You may not be called on right then, but there is no reason to get upset and cause confusion among the members. It should be God's answer anyway on how everything should flow. This is why it is very important to get in a Biblical based church where a God sent pastor who knows the voice of God, obeys and fears God, walks after the things of God, exemplifies a loving and peacemaking spirit himself toward the church body and administration. You can win in your ministry but you must constantly seek after God on making the best choices and how to treat one another daily in order to be victorious and keep the devil out.

If there is conflict, leaving the church is not the answer. Each person should come together, go talk to the pastor or leader in charge, and resolve the matter Biblically, spiritually, prayerfully, and orderly as best as possible. Prayer is always the key to bringing peace in every situation that rises up among the members. Sometimes the conflict is too bad to talk about it, so in this case you should pray and fast about it first, then go to that person or the leader and request a meeting and you all come together and meet about it, pray about it, hear from God on the matter, and come to a peaceful resolution.

Conflict will come, but it is how you handle it when it does. Will you run from conflict and run your mouth uncontrollably? Will you stand up and bold in Christ and say what is not right and not back down or weaken out? Will you obey God in the matter of peace, love and ready to forgive? The questions are important to ask yourself and they require an answer within yourself as you strive to become a better person, a better Christian for Christ, a better leader, a better pastor, and minister, a better deacon, a better deaconess, a better youth pastor, a better youth and young adult leader, a better member to the best that you can be.

Scriptures to Study in this Area:

- Romans 12
- Romans 14
- Romans 14:10-13
- Romans 14:16
- Romans 14:19   *Follow after the things that make peace.*
- Romans 13:13-14

11

Restore One Another in Peace

The Word of God clearly states when a brother or sister is overtaken in a fault (makes a mistake or sins), you which are spiritual (the church, Christians, Body of Christ, Pastor, Church leaders, Christian mother, Christian father, Christian relative, Christian friend, etc.), restore that person in meekness, taking into consideration that you yourself may be tempted and fall too (Galatians 6:1).

You should never uncover your brother or sister's sins, especially when they have counseled or confided in you in secret.

We as Christian Believers should be ready to bear one another's burdens as we fulfill the law of Christ (Galatians 6:2).

You should never get to a place where you think you're all that and that you are something more than everybody else, when you, as the Word of God says, are nothing. You deceive yourself. We all are nothing without Christ; we are all saved by grace as God showed mercy on us for our sins. As

Abraham never put himself higher than he should, for he trusted, believed, and loved God so much that he let God know that he was nothing and could be blown away at any given time (Genesis 18:27). Many times Christians who think of themselves more higher than they should, end up closing the door in the face of a person who is struggling with a sin, and that person turns and goes back to the sin they came from. As a result, they close the door to Christianity altogether. You must be careful as Christian Believers not to judge and to think of yourself more higher and shut out those who need help as if you never sinned and needed help. You may say, "I've never physically sinned, so I do not understand what you are talking about." And I will tell you that the Bible says that we *"all have sinned, and come short of God's glory"* (Romans 3:23). Just because you have never sinned physically, you have thought of something in your mind that was not of God. You sinned in your mind and the Word of God says *"so a man thinks in his heart, so is he"* (Proverbs 23:7). If you think sin, you have sinned. God is no respect of persons. All sin is sin. He has no favorites. So in this case, this should humble you and keep you humble and remind you to love as there was a time when you needed it yourself.

You should never uncover your brother or sister's sins, especially when they have counseled or confided in you in secret. It is a shame when a person goes to someone who they feel that they can trust, and the one they told their business to, betrays them and spreads their business all over the church, the job, their family, other friends, the town, the city, all on the radio, in a book, and so on. We are supposed to be able to go to another trustworthy Christian in the meekness of love and trust and be able to confess our faults (sins) to them and be healed as the Bible declares (James 5:16). However, this is not happening within the Christian faith and the Body of Christ. Your business is somebody else's business and this should not be so. You have to be able to draw the line when someone may ask you about someone else's business and rebuke them by letting them know that you will not share that person's business. When this is practiced, your accountability with God will be deleted and you will not reap what you sowed. Too many are dying and have died because of hurt and betrayal. Be careful who you think you can trust, that person who you are trusting and confiding in about someone else, is the same one that is sharing your business. Make sure you get in prayer and seek God on bringing you a trustworthy friend or faith partner who you can confide in. God would never send you a person who will betray you. This is important to remember.

To be uncovered in an open place is absurd. You should never openly uncover someone who have confessed their faults and sins. You do not realize that what manner of evil you do to others will come back to you (Galatians 6:7). You have to realize that you can be in that same position one day and desperately need someone to cover you. Strive to forgive and to restore your brother or sister in Christ in the spirit of peace and love. It will make a lasting difference and the devil will be destroyed.

12

Peacemaking Wherever & in the Work Place
No Matter What Tom Says
When Tom Has a Problem with Everyone,
Most Likely Tom is the Problem

Ever met a person who complains about everything and blames everything on everybody else? Especially in the work place. This person is considered a Tom. Tom is a fictitious name that represents all of those who think that they are perfect and there is not a wrong bone in their body. This person is someone who is never satisfied and very unhappy with themselves.

It is important to be happy with yourself. No one can make you happy but you.

Ever met a person who contaminates the environment when they come into the room or the work place with their complaining? They completely ruin the mood of happiness and peace that was already there before they came. They strive to ruin everybody's day with the latest negative news and how something is wrong with everybody but them. When Tom has a problem with everybody, usually Tom is the problem. The question you have to ask yourself, are you a Tom? Does this fit who you are? If you complain about everything and there is something wrong with everybody, you can bet that you are the problem. You are right, there is something wrong with everybody because no one is perfect. WE all have hang-ups and something negative about us that WE all wish that WE did not have. Whether it is:

1. A bad attitude.
2. A filthy mouth.
3. Hatred toward someone—do not want to forgive.
4. Lie all the time—cannot be trusted.
5. Lazy and want to lay around all the time.
6. Do not listen to positive instruction.
7. Do not take regular baths.
8. Do not brush your teeth.
9. Bad breath and fail to do anything about it.
10. Heavy weight, too skinny, judge others too much.
11. Busy Body—messing in other people's business.
12. Moves too slow when given instructions.
13. Too slow on projects.
14. Does not listen to instructions. Cannot be led.
15. Negative all the time.

16. Unappreciative.

17. Selfish. Thinks only of yourself.

18. Argumentative.

19. Does not manage money well.

The solution here is to turn all of the negative hang-ups you have into positive outcomes. Such as:

1. A great positive attitude.

2. A mouth filled with encouragement and love. To build up and not tear down.

3. Love everyone—ready to forgive.

4. A truthful person.

5. Motivated and ready to work.

6. Listens to instruction and is great to work with.

7. Great hygiene. Keeps yourself clean regularly.

8. Keeps your teeth clean regularly.

9. Brushes your teeth regularly.

10. Takes your fitness and health serious. Workout regularly. Does not judge, but realize you are not perfect.

11. Minds your own business.

12. Moves quickly right when instructions are given.

13. Moves quickly. Finishes projects before time.

14. Listens to instructions. Can be led.

15. Positive all the time.
16. Appreciative.
17. Unselfish. Thinks of others before thinking of yourself.
18. A peacemaker.
19. Is a very good money manager.

Which one of these are you? Do you represent the negative list or do you represent the positive list? Do people come around you and have a peaceful vibe about you? Do people look forward to being around you again after having a conversation with you? Do you leave a good impression when leaving a room full of people? When watching television and seeing all of the negative things happening around the world, do you speak or think positive as to hope a positive solution will be found, or do you blend in with a bunch of complaints as you add to the negativity?

I have found that it is easy to receive a compliment. However, it is very hard for most to give a compliment. No one wants to tell someone something good about them. A peacemaker strives to compliment every chance they get. Take the challenge to have the best attitude even when you do not feel like it. Try to think positive about everything and everybody when what you may see is unbearably gruesome and negative. Ask others to hold you accountable for your attitude as you turn negative thinking and attitude into a positive thinking and wholesome loving attitude. No one can take this responsibility for you, you must make up in your mind that you will no longer be negative and hateful in thinking toward yourself and toward others.

Try the positive thinking and doing process:
1. I will choose to think lovingly no matter what.
2. I will choose to think something good about everything and everyone.
3. I will choose to think that I can when challenged that I can't.

Tom is a problem seeker, a problem starter, and a problem holder.

Tom _seeks_ to find problems in everybody else. He seeks not to find a positive solution, but seeks to expose the truth in everything and everybody else. I have heard this before, "Do 99.9 positive things right and get no thank you's, but I do .1 thing wrong and they will harp on that one thing." Never happy, never satisfied, and never appreciative for all of the 99.9 things that were done, and celebrate that.

Tom looks to _start_ fights and arguments, which can possibly bring a fight. He literally hates it when everybody is getting along. In fact, he leaves the room when everyone is happy and tries to think of ways to make them unhappy and possibly fight. He seeks to disrupt good. Are you Tom in this area of seeking anything that is not good? Do you seek to make others unhappy? Peacemaking is about seeking a positive solution to every matter. If you are Tom who seeks evil or negative outcomes, turn it around to be as positive as you can.

Tom is a problem _holder_. He holds every wrong that you have done to him. He looks for you to hurt him, rather than look over your faults because he knows no one is perfect and mistakes will happen. His feelings are easily hurt. He holds problems in his heart and remembers every wrong thing that you did to him.

Tom holds his problems in his heart and when he comes around you, he makes you accountable for his problems. His presence soon rubs off on you and contaminates you to a point where you feel his problems and you yourself begin to think about all the problems you have and begin to complain about them. Are you guilty of this? Do you hold your problems within and blame God for every one of them? Do you hold others accountable for your problem that has nothing to do with them? The solution here is to STOP and look at YOURSELF. Take the initiative that you are no longer going to wobble in defeat and hold every single solitary thing within that you are not happy with. Look to release those things that bother you and talk peacefully and sensibly to someone who can help you release. I experienced meeting a person in ministry who was very unhappy and let everybody know who came around them. Their presence was very unpleasing. In fact, they affected the entire ministry and made everyone uneasy. They caused confusion among the leadership and watched everybody hash it out. Soon everybody began to realize who it was that was making all of the commotion and soon prayed that they be removed. It worked, they left the church. Was this an effective way to get rid of that person? How would you have handled them and the situation?

It is important to be happy with yourself. No one can make you happy but you. If you are not happy with yourself, it doesn't matter how hard they try to make you happy, you will never find happiness in any of their attempts. You will always look for them to say or do one damaging thing, which most times the damage comes from you. You damaged them with the way you came off and made them react to that by striking back with a not so pleasing self-defense. You took them as damaging you because this is infested within your heart. When actually you were deceived. The problem lies within you. Your unhappinesss has become a disorder—an inner illness and complaint that no one can fix but God Himself. If you know someone like this or this fits you, seek God right away and release what you are unhappy with, and allow Him to fix it for you. True victory comes when you can be honest with yourself. Come clean with all of the unnatural things you are feeling within yourself. You are the bigger person who has chosen to be a peacemaker first with yourself and then with others.

13

Peacemaking Through the Spirit of Love

When you love, you are imparting something so profound within you and others that no one on this earth can give. You are being a peacemaker when you love. You are exemplifying one of the most important commandments in the Bible — love. This literally transfers on others. When you walk in a room full of quiet boring people, and began to show love to them, they will immediately come alive. I know this to be true. There have been times when others I was around were down and the last thing on their minds were loving

> When you love, you are imparting something so profound within you and others that no one on this earth can give.

someone else other than themselves, which I question as well. I purposely showed them love by saying something that they wanted to hear, cracking a joke I knew they would laugh at, and reaching out by giving them a loving card. This change the course of their day and life, which was headed to the land of dome and bloom. But, when the Spirit of Love came in, it changed their day and life forever.

Jesus Christ was, and still is the greatest example of love. You may ask how? Well, He did one of the most outstanding and breath taking things nobody on this earth would have ever done, He was wounded for all of our transgressions, He was bruised for all of our iniquities, the chastisement was upon Him, He suffered and died on the cross just for our sins, and I cannot leave the fact that He rose again to conquer death and to give each and every one of us who are His children eternal life. He made peace with all man through His Spirit of love. There is no greater love than this but for us all to pan our lives and love walk after Him—constantly making peace with all men.

Being practical, I do not believe that there is no other way around the fact that when you love, you immediately are making a peace connection with that person. You can literally change an evil person's persona. He or she would be forced to bow down and give you what you want when you love and make peace. The Word of God says, your enemies will make peace with you when you love (Proverbs 16:7). You should make every effort to love and to make peace no matter what in order that you might keep out conflict. It should be the goal of every person to make peace so that you may draw an unbeliever to Christ just by your love. I have never heard of someone accepting Christ by someone who was evil and mean to them. I only heard the opposite, they were drawn and they changed from being evil, hateful and received Christ because they were loved. Most times that is all people want is to be loved, and for you to show them how to love so that it will rub off on them to do the same. However, when you never do it, it confuses the unbeliever and makes them wonder if you were ever saved and have a personal relationship with the Lord. You should never want that label on you. You should want to leave their presence with the words on their lips, "I know you know Jesus."

14

The Award Winning Peacemaker
Through the Spirit of Love

As I shared in the previous chapter, Jesus is the greatest example of being the award winning Peacemaker through the bonds of Love. There is no greater love than this, that a man would lay down His life for us (1 John 3:16). Are you really thinking about what this scripture is saying? It is breath taking. It is profound to the core. It cannot be changed or manipulated. It is so.

Jesus is the award-winning peacemaker of them all through love.

Jesus is the award-winning Peacemaker of them all through love. He loves everybody. He loved His enemies. This is something that most of us struggle to do. But we can follow in His footsteps and live our lives as He did. I know you may be saying, "there is no way I can love like Jesus loved because I have been hurt way too bad." I will say to you that none of us can be just like Jesus at all times because He was perfect although tempted, but never sinned. However, you can strive to come as close as you possibly can. You may not always have perfect days, but you make those days that are a challenge for you the best days of your life. You press through the days you want to give up and quit. You shake off the bad news that seems unshakable, or the person who strives to work your nerves to the limit.

Most times you can tell in the morning how your day will be by the way you feel. Say a prayer that God will guide your day and keep all evil away from you and give you a great day. This is a good start. From there be determined to win being a peacemaker through love just as Jesus Christ Himself exemplified. Jesus' days were not always perfect. He had some challenges as we do. One was when the devil came and tempted him in the wilderness (Matthew 4:1-11). Another was when the soldiers came to take him away in the garden (John 18:1-12). Each of these passages of scriptures show that He was having a challenge, but through it all, He trusted God anyway and pressed through it and did the will of the Father. This is the same for you. You have to trust that God will handle everything that tempts you, concerns you, everything you are troubled about, and everybody who comes in your presence who may challenge your love walk.

The Peacemaker Group Discussion Topics

1. How to use conflict as an opportunity to demonstrate the love and power of Jesus Christ
2. When it is appropriate to overlook an offense
3. How to change attitudes and habits that lead to conflict
4. How to confess wrongs honestly and effectively
5. When to assert your rights
6. How to correct others effectively
7. How to forgive others and achieve genuine reconciliation
8. How to negotiate just and reasonable agreements
9. When to ask the church to intervene in a conflict
10. How to deal with people who refuse to be reasonable

The Peacemaker Discussion Questions

Do you consider yourself a peacemaker?

Explain why or why not if you answered yes or no?

How do you plan to be a better peacemaker while in the mist of conflict?

Have you ever had a conflict that did not turn out so good (church, spousal issue, children, family, friends, perfect stranger, on your job, etc.)? What did you do to resolve it?

If you did not resolve the conflict that did not turn out so good, what do you plan to do if a next one should arise?

More in Depth Discussion Questions:
Think of relationships that work. How can you learn from them by watching them and use them with others?

Do you feel that shunning yourself away from everybody is a great way to develop great rewarding and lasting relationships with others? If you are standoffish, how do you plan to become more sociable the winning way that would leave you walking away smiling that there was peace and/or a difference made?

In terms of peacemaking, how does mutual respect and unconditional love play a part in your relationships whether with family, friends, spouse, children, job, staff, co-workers, and passerby's in a store?

Think about the closest person in your life. Do you feel that there is peace between you two and are victorious when or if conflict should arise? How do you handle it if so?

Scriptural Index

Chapter 1
James 1:19

Genesis 4:1-16

Chapter 2
John 15:12

Chapter 3
Proverbs 27:5

Chapter 4
Matthew 21:12-13

Acts 6:1-7

Matthew 17:21

Mark 12:31

1 Thessalonians 5:17

Proverbs 18:24

1 Thessalonians 4:9

Matthew 5:44

1 Thessalonians 5:11-13

Isaiah 53:4-5

1 Corinthians 10:13

Chapter 5
John 18:10-11

James 1:19

Chapter 6
Romans 8:1

Romans 7:15-23

Chapter 7
John 10:10

James 1:19

Chapter 8
Revelation 3:19

Chapter 9
Matthew 18:21-22

Chapter 10
Romans 12

Romans 14

Romans 14:10-13

Romans 14:16

Romans 14:19 *(Follow after the things that make peace.)*

Romans 13:13-14

Chapter 11
Galatians 6:1

Galatians 6:2

Genesis 18:27

Romans 3:23

Proverbs 23:7

James 5:16

Galatians 6:7

Chapter 12

Chapter 13

Chapter 14
1 John 3:16

Matthew 4:1-11

John 18:1-12

ADDITIONAL SCRIPTURES:

Proverbs 16:7

Romans 12:21 be not evil, but overcome evil with good.

Romans 14:10-12 criticizing and passing judgment on your brother
A kind word or answer turns away wrath.

Romans 14:16 let not your good be evil spoken of.

Notes

Contact

Stephanie Franklin
EMAIL: info@stephaniefranklin.org
WEBSITE: www.stephaniefranklin.org

Stephanie Franklin,

M. TH., MDIV

Has obtained her Master of Arts Degree in Theological Studies and in Divinity. She has a heart to reach the youth and young adults along with the entire family, bringing them all together as a unified fold.

Stephanie's mission while on this earth is to be used by God in whatever capacity He chooses.

She enjoys reading, writing, and spending time with family and friends.

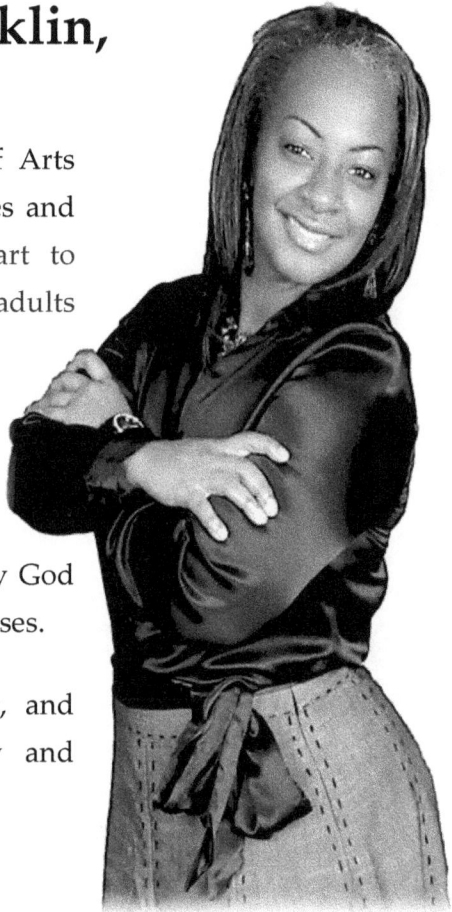

www.ingramcontent.com/pod-product-compliance
Lightning Source LLC
Chambersburg PA
CBHW051732090426
42738CB00010B/2220